FOREX TRADING FOR BEGINNERS BOOK #8

How to Manage the Risk and to Be Profitable in Long Run, Tips and Tricks to Trade Like a Pro

MARK P. ANDERSON

FOREX TRADING FOR BEGINNERS BOOK #8

Table Of Contents

Introduction

For international trade to take place effectively, countries need to have access to a market that enables them to convert local currencies to other currencies. This means that forex trading is an important factor in facilitating trade between different countries. For example, if a company in the United States was to import goods from Germany or any other European country, it can easily pay for the transaction in Euros rather than dollars by converting U.S dollars into euros.

History of Forex Trading

Currency exchange has always been an important part of trade throughout history. It enabled people from different regions to trade in items such as food, cloth, tools, and many other essentials. For instance, if Egyptian merchants were trading with Turkish merchants, and the Turkish merchant's currency was worth more than the Egyptian currency in terms of value, the Turkish trader would be able to purchase more goods with fewer coins because the value of his coins would make them superior in terms of purchasing power.

Throughout history, the value of currencies has been set against commonly recognized measures such as gold or silver. Gold was typically used to fix the value of a currency by providing a measure that could equate a certain quantity of gold to a certain amount of money. Silver was also used as a measure of value for different currencies.

As early as the fifteenth century, banks had been opened to facilitate trade between different countries. The year 1880 is considered the beginning of the foreign exchange, and it saw the establishment of the gold standard. The gold standard meant that the standard economic unit of account was established based on a fixed quantity of gold. This standard was widely used in the 19th century and as well as in the early part of the 20th century.

The increase in the volume called for a better trading system, and this is what prompted Reuters to introduce computer monitors into the forex trading market from 1973. Hitherto the introduction of computers, telephones, and telexes were the main platforms that were used for trading quotes.

By the end of the first quarter of 2010, at least 36% of the trading volume in the forex trading market was attributed to the U.K., making it the largest foreign exchange trading center at the time. The United States, over the same period, accounted for at least 17% of the global foreign exchange trade while Japan was third in terms of volume with a contribution of 6% of the total traded volume.

Recent years have seen a remarkable increase in the total turnover of forex trade. By April 2010, the turnover of the options and futures market had reached the $ 166 billion mark. As it stands, over 2% of OTC turnover in foreign exchange is accounted for by forex currency derivatives.

While there are numerous different currency pairs from all around the world, there are just 18 that is considered by most to be of the greatest importance. While this doesn't mean that you should try and trade all of the pairs at once, it does mean that you will need to be aware of them and what they are doing so you have a better forecast of the market as a whole. Even better, the 18 pairs are all from just eight countries. While this doesn't make successful Forex trading any easier, it will make it easier when it comes to knowing where to put your focus.

CHAPTER 1:

Developing Your Trading Plan

You now have the fundamental principles of Forex trading under your belt, and you are aware of what you are trading in and why. So how do you translate that into a practical application?

Every successful trader enters the marketplace with a clear plan in their mind, and the reason they can then describe themselves as successful is that they follow it dutifully and religiously.

Now, while it's true that you can find software out there that will make those decisions for you, I strongly recommend that you avoid the temptation. Much as with those crash diets that never help lose more than a couple of pounds and the wonder medicines that do little else than taste unpleasant, those software programs tend to be snake oil. After all, if they really did work, everyone would be using them, and everyone would be millionaires.

Instead, you're going to have to create your own plan and then rely on your hard work to research the markets, your intuition, and your ability to assess the risk to provide the rest.

Getting started is relatively simple. You will need to provide yourself the answer to two questions:

- What is the maximum loss you are prepared to make in a single position? (In percentage terms.)

- What will be your stop-loss position on your trades?

Every trader needs to know the answer to those questions, although everything else is fluid and personal. Your ability to analyze the market, the time of day you trade, your capital and risk ability – these things are all distinctly personal, which means there is no possible way to develop a plan that works for absolutely everybody.

Not to mention that the same strategy won't necessarily work in every market and on every trade or with every currency pair.

You will need to develop a fluid mindset that can adapt your plan accordingly to the realities of the market.

So, with that in mind, how do you develop your personal strategy? Start with the two questions above, as these are designed to make sure that the capital in your trading account remains intact.

Answer those questions with a mind to your trading account and to how much you can afford to lose before you no longer have the capital to continue trading.

Your answers are the only ones to which you must adhere religiously, come what may. Consider your capital to be your prized possession and worthy of protection at all times.

A quick example to show you how those questions then apply to actual trade. Let's assume that you've decided that your maximum risk on a trade is going to be $45, which equates to 2 percent of your capital (I would recommend never going above 5 percent), and that you've decided your stop-loss position will represent three times the average pip movement of that currency pair.

Now let's assume you're looking at a trade that moves on average five pips within your chosen timeframe. You would therefore have a stop loss position of 15 pips. If you divide the maximum loss you're prepared to make by the number of pips, you get the number 3, which translates to $3 per pip.

So what does that mean? It means that you want a contract that balances out at $3 per pip.

You can, of course, then play with your equation. For example, if you enter into a contract with less risk than you're prepared to take, you can then increase your position later if your predictions bear out, adding more contracts until you reach that $45 maximum. Don't forget that the answer to these questions represents the maximum risk you're prepared to take, so you don't actually have to meet those numbers exactly as long as you don't exceed them.

Step by Step Trading Plan Decisions

With those two basic questions asked and answered, you have numbers to play with that will guide you through individual trades. But what of your overall strategy? To develop that, you'll need to ask yourself some questions that you may have already been thinking about as you worked through this book.

1. How much capital do you want to invest, and how much time do you want to spend trading? The decisions you make about your trading need to fit with your lifestyle and responsibilities, so it's best to work this out first and then develop your plan to fit around these basic needs.

2. How do you want to perform your analysis? You've been introduced to the basics of both fundamental and technical analysis in this book, and I did suggest that a combination of the two is a good idea. Before you decide which to use, experiment with them for a little while.

Make theoretical trades based on what you have learned through research and see how they pan out. Traders don't all use one or the other of these systems, and that's for a good reason – our brains all work in their own unique ways, and you may find yourself making better decisions using one over the other.

3. What are your financial goals and targets? It's paramount as a trader that you are consistent in your approach, and making sure you have these goals will ensure that you are. As a quick note, your goals should be based on the number of pips you want to gain, not a solid figure in dollars or pounds.
   As your capital grows, you'll be investing in bigger contracts, so the pips will represent larger amounts of money. This is how you will grow your capital: by consistently following the same strategy as you go along and seeing how that strategy brings bigger gains over time.

4. Do you want to be a long or short term trader? This is going to affect how you perform your research and what you are looking for and, ultimately, will dictate what it is that makes you decide to enter into a trade.

5. What currency pairs do you want to trade-in? Keep in mind the risk associated with each pair and also your personal circumstances – there's no point trading on a currency that's barely moving during the time you're able to trade, for example.

With all these questions answered, you must now take on board that all of your tradings are going to come down to the idea of risk. It is based around how much risk you are prepared to take in general – the answers to those first two questions – and how much risk a particular position represents. If you keep this in mind during every trade decision, you can't go too far wrong.

Make those high-risk choices if you want to, but make sure that you're aware they are high risk before you do and that you're not taking any greater risk than your plan dictates.

CHAPTER 2:

Beginners' Mistakes to Avoid

The investor who faces the world of financial markets should be considered as a person who wants to learn how to play tennis. You are obliged to know the rules of the game, have the necessary materials, and attend teacher/student lessons, telling them what they should and shouldn't do. This paragraph and the following paragraph are instead dedicated to the things that should not be done, that is, the mistakes that traders and investors tend to repeat with a specific frequency.

1. **Not Accepting Losses.** One of the biggest problems facing the trader is not to close at a loss trades that prove to be incorrect. It is a difficulty related to both the economic and psychological aspects (many people find it extremely difficult to admit that they have made a mistake). Many traders build operating strategies with stop-loss only "theoretically": that is, they identify a level of support and, mentally, think of closing the position if prices fall below that threshold. Then, when prices actually break the support, and you have to suffer the loss, they prefer to wait for something to change. Some people think the

market is wrong. Others seek some technical motivation to assume that it is just a false signal. Others increase positions to mediate the load price. Nothing more wrong. The truth is that, frequently, the strategy that was built turned out to be wrong, and we need to get out of that position immediately before the situation worsens further.

2. **Not Following Pre-Established Rules.** The lack of an operational plan built at the table, in which you define where it is determined how much to invest in the single operation; what is the maximum risk you are willing to take; what are the operational levels that you intend to use in your operation (entry-level, initial stop-loss, take-profit), lead the trader to make mistakes dictated by the emotionality and stress of having to then manage the position in real-time. Doubts arise, doubts, uncertainties that have nothing to do with the analysis that was carried out in firm bowls and which had led to the judgment as interesting a specific technical situation.

3. **Not Learning From Mistakes.** Often operators make the same kind of error (they enter the market earlier than they should, they get into a late position, close the area soon, they do not comply with stop-loss, and so on), and from their mistakes, they fail to draw due lessons. To be

able to analyze in detail your operations, it is advisable to keep the accounting of the various transactions, marking the entry-level, the stop-loss, the possible take-profit, and the reason for which the transaction was made. Only the correct registration of all trade can allow you to objectively evaluate the results obtained, identifying the situations on which you are profitable and those on which you make mistakes and suffer losses.

4. **Not Being Patient.** One of the difficulties that the trader often encounters is to know how to wait for urgent situations to be created. Staying on standby for a while can be mentally unnerving. This leads the trader to trade even when there are no conditions, just because he has to do something. In some cases, you also risk going into overtrading (i.e., operating frantically, without a basic logic), for the desire to recover prior losses or to want to continue a possible positive streak of operations.

5. **Not Letting Their Profits Run Fast Enough.** One of the basic rules of trading claims to "cut losses and let profits run." When the market goes in the intended direction, it is appropriate (I would say necessary) to exploit the situation, but following pre-established rules (taking partial profit, for example, after prices have made a

favorable movement, proportionate to the initial risk to which you are exposed). One of the techniques that can be used is to simulate your table operation (what in technical jargon is called paper trading) to be able to evaluate whether the targets/take-profits that are used in their operations are too close or too far from the movement made by the market. In some cases, it will be found that you have closed your positions too early, while in others, you have set too ambitious targets.

6. **Not Following Strict Money Management Rules.** Only careful money management can allow financial markets to survive for a long time. The trader who takes too high risks, who does not correctly relate the size of the individual positions to the total capital at their disposal, which does not respect the set stop-loss, is inevitably destined to suffer losses. To achieve positive returns consistently, you need to be extremely disciplined and rigid in your operations.

   If these rules are not followed, inevitably, our equity-line (the cumulative line of profits and losses, which records the outcome of the various transactions) will be very volatile: there will be periods when good results are obtained (however high risk), but also periods in which you suffer substantial losses.

7. **Following Rumors/News Instead of Your Analyses.** Many traders are often distracted by the river of news that is constantly coming into the market and tend to be influenced by the opinions expressed by other analysts. It should never be forgotten that trading means working on prices: the latter must, therefore, be closely followed, analyzed, and studied.

   You have to understand how they formed and what their future behavior might be. Everything else is just "noise" background noise, which can certainly generate volatility (on the occasion, for example, the dissemination of important macro data or as a result of some particularly relevant corporate choices), but it is rarely able to change the technical structure of the market.

   If the latter is set to rise, it will find a way to rise even in the presence of a negative environment (indeed, a market that does not fall when negative news comes is a symptom of strength and indicates the will to rise, with buyers who have exploited this news to accumulate upward positions); if instead the market is set to fall, it will find a way to fall even in the presence of a positive environment (indeed, a market that does not rise when positive news comes is symptomatic of extreme weakness and indicates the willingness to go down, with sellers who have used this news to liquidate any long positions or open new short positions).

8. **Using Complex Analyses.** Novice traders, often in search of the Holy Grail, fill their screens with technical indicators/oscillators, numerous trendlines) that intersect with prices, complex graphical methods that are difficult to decipher. Nothing more wrong. The chart should be as clean as possible, with prices needing to have the highest visibility possible, with some trend lines that help identify the main trend and identify the main levels of support or resistance, and few, very few indicators that can provide useful operational information. The goal is to achieve a chart/layout that is as clear and as simple as possible, where the key levels that have been formed and on which you intend to operate must be evident.

9. **Not Being Clear.** When you decide to open a new position (and therefore put your money at risk), you need to have a clear and accurate picture of the situation. If you have doubts, uncertainties, indecisions, it is better to give up. If the technical picture is mixed, it means that the market itself is undecided about what to do. Under these conditions, it is preferable to stay at the window, waiting for the scenario to clear up or unlock. The basic rule is that we enter the market only when

the probability of success is in our favor, that is, when the analyses conducted (graphical analysis, quantitative analysis, and volumetric analysis) are all agreed in highlighting that prices are destined to rise (for long operation) or to fall (for a short operation). In general, it is preferable to miss an opportunity rather than take a risk by betting that prices will take the desired direction.

Trading only achieves positive results if you take advantage of favorable situations and reduce your level of risk as much as possible.

10. **Changing From One Strategy to Another.** The trader must build a solid analysis methodology and a sound operational strategy. The latter requires you to operate only when there are technical situations that the operator has learned both to recognize (for example, a breakup) or a reversal bar), and to exploit. This means that, in the face of similar situations, you will have to operate similarly, always using the same tools (graphs/quantitative/volumes), taking on the same level of risk, and managing the position in the same way. It is, therefore, not necessary to change the way it operates just because the latest results have been negative.
    Losses need to be managed and analyzed, but they must not make us abandon a methodology that, over time, has proven to work.

CHAPTER 3:

The Trading Strategy

You need a trading strategy to place your trades. You can have all the trading requirements to make you a successful trader, but without the right trading strategy, you won't get any profits at all.

Never start your trades when you do not have a strategy in place.

Developing the Right Trading Strategy

Day trading strategies are important for beginners and advanced traders. The good news is that the process is easy. The bad news is that coming up with the right profitable strategy is harder than you might think.

1. Choosing the Right Market

There are various viable day trading markets that you can explore. These include stocks, Forex, and futures. One of the top questions that new traders ask is, "which is the best market?" Under this heading, we shall look at the different markets and the pros and cons of each.

However, the best market depends on how much money you have, interests, and time. We also look at the potential of each market.

2. Pick a Market You Have a Lot of Interest In

Day trading is tough. No one should lie to you that it is something you can do without all the prerequisites.

When you come across something challenging, the best thing is to have an interest in it. If you aren't passionate about day trading, it is prudent that you put your time into something else.

When starting out, pick a single market and focus on it. Once you have mastered the first market, you can then branch out to other markets, but remember to focus on one market at a time. Trying to learn too many markets distracts you, and you lose out.

Start with the market you have more interest in, stick to it, and build the skills. If you like the market and it is working for you, and then you don't have any reason to trade anything else. Trading multiple markets won't give you more income.

3. Understand the Income Potential

All the different types of markets are giving you the chance to make money out of your trades. Forex, stocks, and futures all give you the same day trading income potential. Therefore, do not think that you will have more money trading futures or stocks with a poor strategy. Thus, income potential shouldn't be your driving force when it comes to choosing a market; instead, you need to check on how much capital you require to enter a particular market. Stocks are more capital intensive than other types of trades. Next is futures followed by Forex.

To trade stocks, you need at least $25,000 in US markets. However, other markets are less stringent, and you can start with even $10,000. However, the US market presents the best for day trading, so it is wise to run trades on it. Many low-level brokers will allow you to open an account with just $1,000 and give you the option to trade at $500. But this isn't advisable because you can't cushion yourself against losses.

Start with enough capital so that you give yourself a fighting chance.

To trade Forex as a day trader, you need to start with preferably $1000 or more so that you can start building an income. Here, many brokers can open accounts for as little as $100.

Remember that all markets have the same profit potential. So, the lesser you invest in any market, the lower the possibility of making money. Just because you can start with a minimum amount doesn't mean you must go with that amount.

When Can You Day Trade?

Futures and Forex markets give you 24-hour periods to trade for 5 days a week. You can actively trade stocks between 9.30 and 4 pm ET.

After you consider which market to trade and how much capital to put in, you also need to look at the time you need to invest in the market. Some times of the day are best suited for trading. Some markets are flexible, with Forex being the most flexible of all of them.

Day trading, especially in currency pairs, offers you the most options when it comes to day trading. Time also matters. For instance, lunchtime isn't a good time to trade.

For day trading stocks, the market usually opens at 9.30 am EST. Sometimes opportunities occur in the hour before this time, but most of the time, the action occurs between 9.30 am and 11.30 am EST.

If you plan to run trades, then focus on them and sit down to actually trade for several hours with total focus. Do not trade from a computer while focusing on another job since you will be distracted.

Look at Market Correlation

If you are using multiple markets to trade, you need to consider the correlation of the markets that you have selected to trade. Products that move together increase the level of risk that you face.

Liquidity and the Risk

The way the market moves is important as well. You need to know the normal trading range per day, the value of per tick, and the volume that is traded each day. You also need to understand the level of liquidity of the order book.

These factors make up the execution risk, which is a factor that determines how easy it is to get in and out of the market at a certain price without too much slippage.

Trade risk refers to what you need to risk to know whether a trade will work out or not.

Selecting a Timeframe

When you decide to go into day trading, you need to choose a timeframe of fewer than 24 hours. Some of the popular timeframes run from 1-minute to 60-minute timeframes. A smaller timeframe gives you smaller profits but low risk as well. Additionally, you have access to more trading opportunities compared to choosing longer timeframes.

When you start day trading, you might want to go for a smaller timeframe to make sure you do not overwork your account. The best timeframe is 15 minutes, which is small enough to capture the best moves and long enough to get rid of any clamor in the market.

However, the 15-minute trend might not work for you the way you want it to do. Make sure you experiment with a lot of time frames so that you choose the best one for your needs. The time frame should also be in line with your trading strategy. For instance, you might find that a plan that won't work on a short timeframe may work on a longer one.

So, start working on your strategy while targeting the shorter time frames, say 15-minute trades, and then change it first before you can change any rules.

Choosing the Right Trading Approach

After you select the right market, you need to choose the perfect trading approach that you would like to use. After this, the fun begins. This is the perfect time for analyzing the various stocks to see which ones are the best investments. You want to determine what each of the companies is all about and what makes its stocks move.

You have to choose between fundamental or technical analysis. Both of these instruments have advantages and disadvantages.

CHAPTER 4:

Risk and Money Management

Budgeting for Profit

Budgeting for profit means that you have to understand how the Forex market works.

If you want to make profits when Forex trading, there are a few tips you can use. For instance, ensure that you start small. This advice applies mainly to those who are new to Forex trading; you can only be successful at trading millions when you have learned how to handle a few dollars as you can be successful in trading dollars when you have learned how to trade pennies. If you are lucky enough to buy many small stocks, there is a probability that they could tremendously increase in value, earning your profits. Luckily, there are traders today who allow you to open an account with just a few dollars. If you constantly use the account, over time, your profits will begin to grow, and you will begin to experience success. Additionally, if you want to succeed, you should be a regular investor. This does not mean you have to put in huge chunks of money for trading each time. It simply means that you could add manageable amounts to your investment every week — for instance, $10 or $20 per week. Being a regular investor not only refines your craft but also grows your account when the profits are compounded over time. When you invest small amounts, you will not feel the pinch, but the rewards will be great regardless.

Another tip when budgeting for profit is to be patient. As has been highlighted above, starting small is a good move. However, many people get frustrated because of the slow process. To enhance your tolerance, trade small, but do not view these small amounts as dollars.

Instead, view them as percentages. If you get a profit of, let us say $1 when you have a $10 account, then you have made a 10% profit.

On the other hand, if you lose a dollar, then you have lost 10%. You will then have learned a valuable lesson about Forex trading at a low cost of just a dollar. Also, when you trade in smaller amounts, you learn to deal with the hurdles associated with learning how to trade Forex.

Risk Management

Risk management involves reducing the size of potential losses while getting the most benefit out of a single trade. Risk management is highly debated as a topic in Forex trading and, yet, it remains important as an aspect of trading because of the volatile nature of the

Forex market. To understand risk management in detail, read on.

One of the fundamental rules of managing risk when trading Forex is to ensure that you only risk what you can afford to lose. Interestingly, many traders make the mistake of investing more than they can afford to lose, especially when they are learning the trade. As a Forex trader, however, you can avoid some of the fundamental mistakes made by traders and become an outstanding trader yourself. You should know when to cut your losses. Cutting losses can be made in two ways. The first is when you impose a mental stop and decide that the right thing to do would be to limit the drawdown, then you can take on a trade. Another way to control losses is by using a trading platform that allows you to lock in stops when your losses reach a particular level.

To control risks, you can also use the correct lot sizes. When accounts are advertised by brokers, they make it seem like a good idea to open an account with, let us say, $300 and use leverage to enhance mini-lot trades. They make it look like this technique will help double your money in just a single trade. This kind of thinking can sometimes deviate from reality. As a new trader, it is important to start small so that you have many options for managing the trade.

You should also be able to track your overall exposure. Reducing lot size is a good step to take. However, other steps, such as opening many lots with currency pairs, could have serious implications. For instance, when you go long on USD/CHF and short on EUR/USD, you are exposed twice to the realities of the dollar movement. Should the dollar tumble, you will suffer double losses, which can be painful. If, however, you keep your exposure limited, you have a better chance at reducing risk and increasing your chances for success in the future.

Trading with a plan is also essential. This is because when you have a plan, you can easily avoid emotional responses, which are a natural part of trading Forex. Having a trading plan will help you know what steps to take from the beginning to the end of your trading session before you open a position. An additional benefit of trading with a plan is that it will keep you from speculations and possible overtrading as a result of there being an open position. Understand that in Forex, you have to have strong will power. Your trading plan is not going to work magically. You must have a plan and follow it to the letter for this risk management strategy to be effective. Another risk management strategy that you can employ is understanding the nature of the currency pairs you have decided to trade. Understand the events scheduled to take place in the day and even week ahead and how the data looks. Look at your trade plan's time horizon and consider liquidity conditions. Have a clear view of what the market has priced in and out because anticipating market events can alert you of possible disruptive circumstances even if it is not a complete indicator of how you can win a trade. By understanding that risk varies across currency pairs, based on different factors such as liquidity, data sensitivity, and volatility, you will be better placed to understand the analytical tools and strategies that are best for you.

Also, you can trade with an edge. This means that you do not have to be in the market all the time despite the fact that the currency market operates round the clock. Block the noise, and do not let it pull you in. You can do this, for instance, by picking a spot and timing yourself. Also, look for setups in which there is a clear risk/reward scenario to avoid an unnecessary headache. Being an opportunist in the real world can be a problem, but that does not mean this strategy cannot work in the digital world of Forex trading. You can take your time looking at the coming trade opportunities and use these chances instead of getting caught up in the market moves of a single moment.

I look forward to future opportunities because there will be more opportunities, and it pays to be ready.

Sometimes in life, it is good to take a step back from situations because it provides an individual with moments of clarity. Therefore, it is advisable to occasionally take a step back from Forex trading. Yes, this means that you need to take time off from the markets completely for a while, and no, you will not miss out on important trades. On the contrary, when you take this break, you may find that it was much needed, you are more objective when you trade, and you have a clearer perspective that keeps you from emotionally investing in a market position. Also, you can use this downtime to develop other skills, such as your understanding of fundamental analysis and to prepare yourself for fresh trading opportunities.

It is important that as a trader, you take your profits regularly. When you take your profits, you are, in essence, reducing your exposure to risks in the market. You may find that your trade plan has an aggressive profit target but imagine what would happen if events do not play in your favor. It is, therefore, a better idea to protect what you have already worked for. After all, nobody has ever gone broke while making a profit.

This is a tactic that can be referred to as taking money off the table. If you keep your profits in your margin account, you are likely to be subject to future trading decisions and are susceptible to unknown risks. Taking money out of your account keeps you in a position where you can trade in comfortable sizes. As you trade, remember that trading is not purely a game of profits.

You can use the profits you make to do other things. For example, you can invest the profits into another venture once you withdraw them.

Additionally, you should ensure accuracy by double-checking. By now, you must have understood that currency trading takes place in a fairly fast-paced environment. It is even faster, thanks to electronic trading. There is, therefore, the risk of human error when inputting orders and trades, and this may have serious implications for you as a trader. For instance, what would be the benefit of putting in place a stop-loss order if it not entered for the right amount of currency? Make it a part of your routine to double-check your order and trade entries to avoid unnecessary mistakes that may prove costly to your Forex trading venture. Ideally, it would be good to double-check figures when you enter them and just before submission. Mistakes happen, but this does not mean you need to let minor errors become the source of your downfall.

Leverage

By now, you must have an idea of what leverage is and what it can do for you in Forex trading.

In Forex, leverage can be described as the ratio of the trader's funds that you are allowed to use to the size of the broker's available funds. In essence, leverage is whatever capital you borrow to increase your returns.

In reality, the leverage size usually exceeds invested capital to a large extent. Leverage is not fixed in all companies and may largely depend on the trading conditions provided by the Forex brokers. You are using leverage can sometimes be a risky affair because, just like a double-edged sword, it may work to your favor or not. Below, we highlight how leverage works and how it can affect your bottom-line.

CHAPTER 5:

Beginners' First Investment

In the midst of the recent investment boom, the number of people who want to effectively increase their own assets by investing in financial products such as stocks and Forex (Foreign Exchange Margin Trading) is increasing very much.

However, it may be difficult for beginners to invest in high-risk assets all of a sudden. So, you should start by improving your skills with index funds.

It is also true that many people think that asset management is very difficult. There are so many terms to learn, and it's a very difficult choice to learn from and what kind of financial products to buy. Especially for those who are not so bright in finance or the economy, it may be difficult at first. This anxiety should be even higher because it could severely damage valuable assets. In such a case, let's consider the purchase of the mutual fund managed by a professional fund manager by all means.

A professional fund manager will choose the best combination of financial products from around the world on your behalf. Among investment trusts, index funds are highly recommended as products that investment beginners should purchase for the first time.

This is a product that invests in indicators that we frequently hear, such as the Nikkei Average, TOPIX, and the Dow In New York.

As you invest, you always need to understand these indexes. That's why it's very useful for beginners to learn about economics and investments. The characteristic of index funds is that commodity prices are determined in conjunction with various indicators in the economy.

Index funds make their investment decisions easier to understand than individual stocks, and price movements are much more stable. Therefore, anyone can easily invest. When purchasing and managing such index funds, it is not so much the profit trend of individual companies as the movement of the global economy as a whole.

Learning in a field called macroeconomics becomes very important. Stock prices will change significantly due to economic indicators and policy announcements from major countries, including Japan. It is very important to properly assess the linkage between daily news and stock prices and to conduct training to properly understand what kind of stock price movement will be made when it comes out.

This knowledge of the economy as a whole is essential for investing. Investment beginners first organize their knowledge in this field in a body-shaped manner and then learn about investment and stock price linkage by purchasing an index fund linked to macro indicators.

Index funds have ETFs (listed mutual funds) on similar products, but the risk is very low because the price movement is milder than that. For stable and wonderful asset management, it is very important to start with such an index fund.

Financial instruments are more or less subject to fees. Financial products pursue returns, but of course, there are risks. It doesn't make sense to risk and offset the revenue you earn with commission costs. You can enjoy making your own investment by reducing the financial burden as much as possible.

Investment trusts may incur a fee of several percent at times. Recently, there are many products called no-road funds that do not charge a fee, so it is important to make effective use of this.

I think many people start their own investments from mutual funds, but surprisingly, it is the fees and costs of mutual funds. Since it is very expensive for a general mutual fund, it is necessary to check the product guidance called the prospectus about financial products at the time of purchase and to confirm the cost of the fee, etc. properly.

We should think about this point properly and make investments that are a little less wasteful. The main principle in long-term investment is that not wasting a small amount of profit leads to significant profits. If you are like this, let's consider using no-road funds as a priority.

With no-road funds, you can not waste money on your investment strategy. The main feature of no-road funds is that there is no commission at the time of purchase, and such products are increasing rapidly in the market.

In general investment trusts, there are purchase fees that occur at the time of purchase and commissions, such as trust fees deducted monthly. The purchase fee can be as high as a few percent at times. Investors must make more money than this fee when they ultimately make a sale. It is a natural idea to purchase products with a low commission.

In addition, trust fees are the costs deducted monthly. If you think about long-term holding, this is nothing better than cheap. In the midst of intensifying competition, various products are appearing on the market more and more. It is a gateway to investors who are wise to choose products with low commissions on the premise of long-term holdings.

Let's think about how to do our best to make as much money as possible. By choosing a mutual fund that is paid a no-road and monthly distribution, you can manage assets stably.

It is very important not only to be blinded by the profits of your asset management but also to have a proper awareness of risks and costs. Considering the relationship between cost and return, it is important to give proper consideration to fees.

Mutual funds vary from product to product, but it is also one of the great pleasures because it contains an amount close to the dividend called a distribution. The timing of dividends varies depending on the product, such as once every month, every other month, or once every six months. If you are investing in distributions, let's carefully consider the span of such payments. It is a very important method of asset management to make your investment more and more efficient in mutual funds. Distributions are a very important source of revenue. Let's use it as a reference when you enjoy thinking about your investment. It also compensates for losses incurred due to lower prices, so you should make good use of them. Some profits rise in price as a major advantage of mutual funds, but there are also dividends and distributions.

You can get both income gain and capital gains mentioned earlier, and the market can compensate for unrealized losses with distributions. Let's enjoy both sides and increase investment efficiency more and more.

Distributions are paid at different times, depending on the product. The timing and number of distributions paid depend on the product. There are a lot of products that the distribution enters every month in the inside, too. Have fun incorporating distributions into your investments. The fund which the distribution enters every month feels very advantageous.

If you hold such a fund for a long time, you can manage your own assets at a very reasonable time. To make investments aimed at distributions, it is important to invest from a long-term perspective.

Again, the important idea is the dollar cost averaging method. It is very important to think about appropriately diversified investment in your asset management from a long perspective. It is very important to protect your assets over a long period. Let's enjoy and do wonderful asset management.

As for the payment status of the distribution, you can easily find it by examining the product. Let's make fun of investment, including distribution, by taking advantage of the advantages of mutual funds that can easily invest in various products around the world.

Stock investment is very risky. If you think about such dangers enough, by incorporating mutual funds well into your usual investments, you can make reliable investments while successfully enjoying the benefits of distributions and other benefits.

If investment trusts are incorporated into asset formation regularly, you can make more reliable investments on your own while making effective use of distributions and other materials.

CHAPTER 6:

Needs to Know About Forex Trading

Forex trading is an avenue that is making people earn a more significant income. There are many platforms where you can put that little penny in the trading and amerce that profits. However, it needs you to be that wise speculator who knows who reads the indicator promptly and knows the point to make that trading. Remember that forex trading is all about the trading of currencies. Therefore, you have to be knowledgeable about how the different currencies perform. The following are the basics where a beginner should know.

You should first be interested in knowing how the currencies behave in the market. That is where one ought to recognize the values of different currencies. The major currencies traded across the globe shows significant value in the market. Some of these currencies include the Us dollar, pound sterling, Swiss franc, Japanese yen, and the euro. That is not to say that other currencies are not traded, but this one has the commanding value in the forex exchange. Therefore, it requires the broker and the trader to be updated on the value of the stated monies. This is because, in some instances, the currencies may deteriorate and increase their worth significantly. Another thing to contemplate is how the paired currencies behave with each other. For example, in the forex chart, you may see the Us dollar combined with the euro or any other pair.

Another thing you ought to know is the type of indicators available and how one can make trading. These indicators follow specific movement criteria. First and foremost, before knowing that indicator thinks of the scales used in the chart. The chart represents a graphical diagram with both the independent and the depend scales. The independent scales are normally plotted on the horizontal axis and the dependent scale on the vertical axis. Therefore, you have to know the different variables in trading. Some of these variables are the price movement, the volume, and many others. Check on these charts ad test the movement of these variables appropriately.

Concerning the indicators, you should be aware of how these indicators behave. They are of different types and are influenced by the variables you use. For a beginner, it is essential to have that knowledge of how they behave is crucial. You have to know the different types of these indicators so that you can follow their trend. Think of the indicators like the Moving Average Convergence and Divergence. This indicator measures the two exponential moving averages. There is the Bollinger band indicator that measures the standard deviation of those currencies of the currencies. In some terms like the volatility market, you also need to know them. Remember that the volatility of the currency is its behavior to have either a sharp increase or decrease in the market. That is where you can either gain a sizable profit or loss.

That is not to forget the relative strength index, which is beneficial for ascertaining the overbought and the oversold. These indicators are very many in particular, but when you have their information is nothing that should stop you from earning—even the types of charts like the candlesticks. Line charts and bar charts should be at your fingertips.

There are different charts for every level of your trading. For example, in your case, as a beginner, you can use the thence stick or the basic charts. Another thing is the trend analysis. You should analyze the direction in which the indicator flows whenever you make a trade. That should help you in analyzing the peak times and recession periods of a paired currency. You also can anticipate the next performance of the paired currency if you are experienced in reading the behaviors of the indicators.

You still use this information to know the right point of the market entry and the exits of the point—those brokers who analyze the trend accordingly and are in a position of obtaining a sizeable return.

Which Qualities Make You a Successful Beginner in Trading?

After knowing the basics, you do not just start trading when you have the minimal qualities required in this business. You will realize how you will get frustrated when you stake a lot of cash, then the trading fails. At other junctures, you need to apply essential speculation tactics. That is the knowledge of probability and analyzing the statistics for you to stand a chance in trading. Some of these qualities are:

Be That Guy Who Is Good in Decision Making. Remember that the facility needs intelligence and critical thinking. You may find yourself succeeding a lot in a particular segment of trading. However, not to realize that it may be a trap where even after making sublime returns, you will eventually gain a hefty loss. Some other times you need not consider only short-term profit but fight for long-term returns.

You may identify a promising venture but where whose returns are realized on a long-term basis. However, if you are that person who needs quick money, you will not be patient on that venture but look for short term profits. Moreover, those who take time in making a decision realizes a pattern trend and make the right move.

Be That Risk-Taker Who Does Not Fear to Make a Loss. If all people were risk-averse, then there would be no forex trading. Hey, remember that this business is like a gamble. I am sure that many people do not like hearing this term, but whenever you are dealing with uncertainties, you are gambling.No matter what you do, you have to sacrifice that penny expecting two possibilities, which are either a win or a loss. Even other renowned investors cite that 'you have to stake big to win big.' Therefore, be a risk-taker who stakes big and hopes for massive earnings of returns. Even if you fail seldom, do not give up, but eventually, you will win.

Be Persistent. When you are persistent, you normally are tolerant. You never give up hope even after failing many times. While your needs are learning from your mistakes, do not repeat the same strategy you did, which failed you. Be that person who sees the failure as a lesson to improve their ways of staking. Adopt a trial and error strategy, which will eventually give you a winning edge. You do not expect to keep winning all the time. You will undoubtedly lose in some instances. You will realize you will keep developing tactics of trading with this trial and error strategy. You will, too, familiarize yourself with the trend analysis, and, therefore, with what is stopping you from knowing how to make that currency trade.

Timing Is Also Operational in the Business. You have to flexible enough to identify a profitable opportunity. The way the currencies behave is like a pendulum that goes in every direction; you can use a stopwatch and identify the specific time the trading signals a return and risks or an entry point and an exit point, because those seconds or minutes you waste may be the advent of your failure. Make a demo trade in which you do not have to input some cash, look at the behavior of the currency, and how they react in any substantial change. You may identify the correct timing when you need to stake, and, therefore, you will have that confidence to risk your money in the trading.

Intelligent Speculation Is Required for This Job. This trading requires you to be wise in reading the trends and having a knowledge of statistics and probability. Those brokers are reputable in making the wise traders are the one who clearly predicts the next behavior of the trading because their experience in reading the scales and indicators further enhances effective trading. Intelligence speculation is a skill that is learned by various strategies, and one of those strategies is the trial and error method, where you will consequently have that experience of trend analysis. Knowledge of the different currencies, charts, and indicators gives you that winning margin. Lastly, you can consult specialists to train you about the analysis of currency trading.

Adequate Preparation Is Needed in This Exercise. How best can you be in a particular exercise if you are not that fully prepared? You must be that person who is willing to set your record straight. Efficient preparation starts with the person who keeps the trading records and can analyze the performance of the currencies using them. Always appreciate the usage of the demo account in which you practices trading. In this, you are not fearful of losing your cash. Once you are used to frequent rehearsals, you are comfortable with making the trading.

What Are the First Steps for a Beginner in Trading?

First, you have to have good preparations. Trading does not fall on the moon; however, you need to have the gadgets for trading. You need to have that electronic device. It can be either your phone, laptop, eye pad, or any other gadget. Make sure you have the best source of the internet because you need to make many references to the currencies from the network. Make sure you are comfortably sat and good to go.

Choose the best agency company in forex trading. Remember, there are many companies online that broke those currencies. To get such firms, one must conduct an extensive study of them. You also need to consider if they are registered and licensed. Moreover, consider their brokerage fee and their essential features. It should have the necessary charts, variables, and indicators which must satisfy the trader. Consult other traders to recommend you the best brokerage firm. When you are satisfied with this, create an account with them. Assess they provide a demo account that is necessary for the trading rehearsal.

The demo account is very vital for you to practice trading. Remember, you cannot put your money in a venture that you do not know; therefore, you must understand it first. If you are satisfied with it, then start the trading program. The good thing with the demo account is that you are not afraid of any risks since you have not staked any cash. Check at the trading platform and its chart.

Open the chart or the diagram and try to choose the currency pair. Most of the time, the currencies are found in the top of the graph, its sides, or below the chart. Look at the available currencies and think about them. You have to be keen in choosing the pair. You can even research how the values of different currencies and how they behave with each other. Do not forget to check their volatility and how they fair when traded. Choose those pairs and fix them at the graph.

CHAPTER 7:

How Can Beginners Manage the Risk?

Forex trading is quite similar to stock investing. The higher the amount of money you invest, the greater your potential profit or loss will be. In currency trading, you need to invest in making a profit. Drawdowns—a decline in a fund or an investment—also happen in currency trading. If you have limited funds, losing a lot will make it hard for you to get back on track.

It is common for beginners to think that Forex trading is easy and fast. But, in truth, becoming good at trading currencies and making profitable trades requires patience, knowledge, time, and commitment.

You also need to consider your broker's trading conditions.

Risk management is integral in Forex trading because the market is unpredictable. Risks can make you lose your capital.

Speculators are the most vulnerable to trading risks. This is because they tend to invest more than what they can afford.

The use of risk management in currency trading separates successful traders from the people who deplete their trading account. When you can manage existing trading risks properly, you can control the amount of capital you can lose on a Forex transaction. Even if you experience the worst-case scenario in a trade, you won't go bankrupt.

1. Only Invest Your Excess Money

This is the very first unwritten rule in Forex trading: Only risk the money that you can afford to lose.

Many beginner traders believe that their first few trades will bring in extra cash.

However, like seasoned traders, beginners will experience losses if they trade carelessly. If you trade using your monthly budget, stop right there! Forex trading is inherently risky. Don't take risks by using the money for your basic necessities.

2. Your Risk/Reward Ratio Should Be Set at 1:3

RRR is an essential tool in currency trading because, as a Forex trader, you have to mitigate and eradicate downside risks.

The RRR helps you set your take-profit and stop-loss orders based on your preferred risk tolerance. Although the ratio depends on every trader, the RRR of 1:3 is the most widely used. With this, you can earn three times as much as your capital.

For example, if the difference between your entry-level and stop-loss order is 20 pips and the distance between your Forex entry point and take-profit is 60 pips, then your risk\reward ratio is 1:3. This implies that you're willing to risk 20 pips to get 60 pips.

3. Maintain the Risks

If you can't completely eradicate a risk, then it's advised to just maintain it. The majority of beginners will increase their investments after making a profit in earlier trade.

If luck is on your side, you can win big by risking everything. However, this is the best way of wiping your trading account clean.

Three winning streaks don't mean that your next trade will be successful. As a beginner, you have to study the trends, the price movement, and the reasons behind your success.

If you become an expert in predicting future prices, and you have an eight-five percent win-rate, only then should you try investing all of the funds in your trading account.

Beginners like yourself should always trade like you're making your first-ever Forex trade. Don't include your gains in your investment.

4. Control and Understand Leverage

Foreign exchanges are leveraged markets. Because of margin trading and leveraging, you can borrow money more than your capital investment.

As collateral, the broker or financier will only ask you to set aside a small percentage of your entire trading account.

When leveraging, you'll make huge profits. If you only make $30 per trade with your $500 trading account, you can earn $90 by borrowing $1000. This strategy is best combined with the 1:3 RRR.

5. Two Percent Investment

As a beginner, the best tactic you can do to manage the risks is to invest only a small percentage of your account on each transaction. By doing so, you can avoid losing streaks and prevent a huge drawdown in your trading account. This can kill your account and make it difficult to reach breakeven. It’s recommended to only trade two percent of your account.

CHAPTER 8:

Secrets to Be Profitable in Long Run

Finding Success in Forex

Since you understand the basics of Forex Trading, you are ready to learn the strategies that traders use to attain success on the market—understanding what you are attempting to accomplish with your trades as well as appreciating that less is more when it comes to trading. Before we jump into the strategies that will aid you in turning a buck in currency trading, let's just spend a moment reiterating some of the important concepts that have led us to this point. There are many key points that you need to understand before you even start talking about strategies.

Successful Trading Strategies

When all is said and done, you are the one responsible for turning your venture into foreign exchange into a successful endeavor. That is actually one of the great things about forex. You do not have a boss screaming down your neck, telling you to do something that you do not agree with. You can come up with your own trading plan based on your research and your knowledge. That being said, success can come more quickly for some than for others, and a lot of the time, this has to do with approaching this endeavor with the right strategy.

Strategy 1. Buy Low and Sell High

If you began currency trading today with $25,000 in your pocket and access to a trading platform, all ready and raring to go, how would you know what is low and what is high? It's your first day. Naturally, for you to understand what would represent a good low investment and conversely what is high, you need to have some knowledge of the exchange rate history of that currency.

Maybe the exchange rate for Japanese yen seems low, but actually, compared to last year or a few months ago, it's a little high. Now it would not be the right time to buy.

Maybe the pound seems low right now, but yesterday the British government announced that the first round of the Brexit negotiations with the EU failed, and therefore, the pound may have room to go lower than it is when you logged onto your trading platform.

Maybe you should wait and see what the pound is later today or tomorrow and buy then. The point here is that buying low and selling high requires understanding the patterns associated with that currency and what might cause it to go up or down, and that's merely the buying side of things. Once you have bought low, you need to figure out when you are going to sell. This is where a good trading plan will come into play. A good plan will prevent you from selling too soon, or even not selling soon enough.

Strategy 2. Focus on Not Losing Money Rather Than On Making Money

This may not be an easy strategy to understand initially, in part because not losing money and making money seem like two sides of the same coin. They are, but they are not identical. One of the personality types that is associated with difficulty in finding success in trading is the impulsive type.

This type of person wants to make money, and they want to make it quick. They have a vague strategy about how they plan on doing that, but the most important thing to them is that they have a high account balance to make as many trades as they need to turn a profit. This is the wrong approach because currencies are not the same as stocks.

The value of a currency may change very little even over a week, so a strategy that involves a lot of trades to make money is usually not the best strategy. You want to have a crystal clear idea of when you are going to but, yes, because you want to make money, but mostly because you don't want to lose. Every market that involves exchanges, like the stock market, has some implicit risk, and currency trading is risky, too, because you may be tempted to give up the advantage you have to try and make money quickly.

Strategy 3. Develop a Sense of Sentiment Analysis

Alright, the third strategy was going to be about Fibonacci retracement, which is a type of technical analysis of the market, but as this is the basics of currency trading, we are going to go into a different strategy that is not any easier than a Fibonacci retracement, just different.

Sentiment analysis is a term that is used in many different specialties, not just finance, and it is not easy to describe. It is essentially a type of analysis that is not based on a chart showing exchange rates over time (technical analysis) or on an understanding of a factor that might today be affecting the value of a currency (fundamental analysis). Sentiment analysis attempts to gauge the tone of the market, the direction the market is heading in by parsing all of the available information.

A key to understanding sentiment analysis is likening it to public opinion. The economy may be booming, people have more money in their pocket, so the currency of this hypothetical country should increase in value, but maybe it doesn't. Maybe there is something that is causing the market to be bearish and which, therefore, might cause the currency to drop. As you perhaps can tell, as this analysis is not based on any concrete information, it can be thought of as intuitive, and no one has intuition on day 1.

Let's just be honest about that. Intuition comes from experience. But the purpose of this strategy is to introduce to you the idea that not the foreign exchange market, like any market, is not going to behave like a machine because it's not a machine.

Markets are places where human beings come together, and humans are unpredictable, often in a frustrating way. Perhaps one day, currency trading may be handled by machines (that wouldn't be fun), but that day is far off, and so you will have to develop your own sense of where the market seems to be going and use this as a strategy to achieve success in this endeavor.

CHAPTER 9:

Tips and Tricks to Trade Like a Pro

Throughout this book, you have been able to learn some of the basic skills that will enable you to make it in the Forex market. However, that alone is not enough. To be an exceptional Forex trader, you have to be equipped with some tips and tricks that will enable you to maneuver around. You have to learn that the best traders are disciplined and practice a lot. They don't just do trade analysis but also perform self-analysis to clearly understand what motivates and drives their trade. By doing a self-analysis, you will also help you to keep both greed and fear out of the trade equation. Here are some of the essential skills, tips, and trips that will make you trade like a pro:

Begin By Defining Your Goals

Before starting your journey as a Forex trader, it is important to have a clear idea about what you would like to achieve and how you intend to get to this destination. Ensure that you have clearly drawn your goals and mastered them in mind. After defining your goals, try to assess through the different trading methods available. Select the best method that fits you and ensures that this trading method will enable you to achieve your set goals. This is because each trading method has its own risk profile, which will require you as a trader to develop some attitude as well as an approach to be a successful Forex trader. For instance, if you are this type of person whose instincts do not allow you to go to sleep when there is an open market position, clearly, you are the best fit for day trading. However, if you are this type of person who is ready to take time and wait for some periods for trade to appreciate, then you are the best fit to be a position trader. It is appropriate that you be sure of your personality. Your personality must fit your trading style. Forex trading at times is stressful; thus, be sure that your personality matches the method of trade you have chosen.

Choosing a Broker and a Trading Platform

It is appropriate that you chose a reputable broker. I advise that as a beginner, start by taking a considerable amount of time to do deep research on the differences between the available brokers. Try to understand the different policies that each broker has, as well as how each of these brokers goes about making a market. You have to understand that doing trade in the over-the-counter market differs from exchange driven market. Again, I advise that you be sure of the trading platform your broker is using to know the suitable analysis that will fit you. For instance, if you trade by analyzing

Fibonacci numbers, just ensure that the platform your broker is using also supports the drawing of Fibonacci lines. Try to understand good brokers with poor trading platforms, poor brokers with good trading platforms, and good brokers with good trading platforms. Ensure that you choose a good broker with a good trading platform.

Before Moving to Multiple Currency Pair, Focus More on One Currency Pair

By now, I believe that you have noted that the Forex trade world is complicated. This is probably attributed to the mixed-up nature of the currency market, the different goals different participants have, and the wide and diverse characters. Unless you are a genius, it will be very difficult to understand all the financial and economic activities going around the world. Therefore, to be a successful Forex trader, you must try to stick your Forex trade activities with the currency pairs you are familiar with and have a good understanding of. It is an even greater advantage if you start with your nation's currency. However, if this is not what you want, I prefer that you chose the widely and most liquid traded currency pairs.

Clearly Determine Your Entry and Exit Points

Often many beginners are usually confused by the information presented in the charts in the different timeframes. This is due to the scenario that most of the time, the information presented in these charts are so conflicting.

There are times when what is shown on the weekly chart as the buying opportunity can be shown up on the intraday chart as a sell signal. It is advised that as a Forex beginner, if you have chosen to shift your trading to a daily chart, say from a weekly chart, ensure that you synchronize these two charts. What I mean is that, suppose your weekly chart gives a buy signal, be patient for the release of a daily chart to confirm a similar signal. Just be sure to keep your timing in sync.

Study the Forex Market and Its Fundamentals

Having a deep understanding of the fundamentals of the Forex market and the technical factors affecting the price action is of great importance. Without a reasonable understanding of the Forex market, you are likely to be affected negatively. However, don't be afraid of the consequences of erroneous application or the consequences of failing to understand the technical or fundamental studies. Learning is a gradual step, and as we make errors, we get to learn more.

You must have proper money management skills as well as emotional skills as these play an important role in the analysis. It is also appropriate that once you make profits, learn how to protect them. I suggest that if you have no skills in money management, learn. Money management will teach you how to minimize your losses and maximize your profits.

I prefer that you develop a bible of money management and put it as a trading library's centerpiece. This will guide you on ways of ensuring that you don't gamble with the profits you have earned hardly as well as cut your losses short.

Be Sure To Calculate Your Expectancy

Basically, expectancy will help you to determine your system's reliability. It is advised that as a trader, you should try to roll back and check your trade history. From here, get a measurement of your winning trades and losing trades. Try to compare the profitability of your winning trades versus the loss of the losing trades. For instance, you can have a look at the last ten trades you have made. Suppose you have not yet made any actual trades, I advise that you go back on your chart. Try to check whether the trading activities would have resulted in losses or profits. Now proceed to total the winning trades found and then divide this total wins.

The below formula will guide you:

Expectancy (E) = $[1+ (L/W)] \times P - 1$

Where we have W and L as the average of the winning trade and losing trade respectively and P being the winning ratio percentage

Case Example

Having made ten trades, out of these ten, you have won 7 and lost 3. The percentage win ratio is [(10-3)/10], which is equivalent to 7/10 (70%). Suppose that these seven trades earned you $4,200, your average win will be ($4,200/7) = $600. Again suppose your losses summed to $1,500, the average loss in the ten trades made will be [$1,500/ (10-7)] = $500. Now apply the use the formula we used to get the expectancy.

E = [1+ (600/500)] x 0.7 - 1

E = [1+1.2] x 0.7 - 1

E = [2.2] x 0.7 -1

E = 1.54 - 1

E = 54%

This means that your system is likely to give you a positive 54% expectancy, and your expected return will be about 50 cents per dollar you invest.

Always Begin With Small Sums

The best tip for any Forex trader wishing to be a professional trader is by beginning with a small account and then increase the size of your account through profits. Don't start by investing heavily. Don’t be confused by the idea that larger accounts will lead you to greater profits. It is perfect when you are able to increase your account size through trading choices. Otherwise, I don’t see the need of you pumping money to an account that will only lead you to strain your finances and emotions.

Focus On Minimizing Losses

Once you have decided to invest in Forex trade and you have funded your account, in your mind, your money is at risk. Therefore, avoid making this trading money to be money used for your regular living expenses but rather look at it as vacation money. Develop an attitude in you that directs you towards trading. With this attitude, you will be psychologically prepared to accept small losses. This is a basic step in risk management. A trader who gives their focus on trade and accepts small losses are more successful than those who focus on constantly counting their equity. To be a professional trader, you must recognize the available markets. However, to recognize the markets, begin by first recognizing yourself. Assess yourself and be aware of your capital allocation for Forex, as well as your tolerance to risks. Just ensure that they are not lacking or excessive. You have to master your financial goals and understand why you are engaging in Forex trading.

Be Motivated By Positive Feedback Loops

By having trade plans that are well executed, you definitely will create a positive feedback loop pattern. As always, success breeds success. You will feel confident when the trade is profitable.

Furthermore, take losses but ensure that they are small according to your trade plan. This will help you build a positive feedback loop.

Be Consistent With Doing Weekend Analysis

The Forex markets are usually closed on the weekends. When closed, take your time to have a deep study on the weekly charts to identify the patterns or news that can have effects on your trade. For instance, you may notice that a particular trade pattern is indicating a double top, but the new and pundits, on the other hand, are making suggestions that there will be a reversal in the market. In the real sense, this kind of reflexivity could only be there to promote some pattern prompting the pundits to reinforce it. Therefore, be patient and, according to your best plan, set up your things and follow your objectives.

Always Keep A Printed Record

When I began doing Forex trading, I always printed all the trade charts. Printed records provided me with a great learning tool. I would, therefore, advise you as a beginner to always print out the charts and then list all the reasons as to why you are making the trade. List the fundamental reasons you feel swayed your decisions. In your printed chart, mark your entry and exit points. Also, ensure that on the chart, you include emotional reasons for taking the actions you took. For instance, if you were anxious, panicked, or you were just greedy, put them all there. By objectifying your trades, you will be able to develop strong mental controls as well as a discipline that will guide you in executing a trade in accordance with your system and not your emotions of personal habits.

CHAPTER 10:

10 Achieving Goals In Forex Trading

With all said and done, there are rules to abide by for one to reach their potential and, most importantly, realize their potential. Below are 10 rules that help in achieving goals in Forex Trading.

1. Trust the Process

Forex trading is a business, and it takes time to grow and be stable, which means that there is more than just waiting for profits. Profit oriented businesses end badly mainly when a forex trader does not meet the threshold they had set, and it is a bad approach for any business. Any business is not only buying and selling as it involves huddles and logistics to make the whole institution work and doable. Money oriented forex traders tend to give up easily when they do not meet their target at the close of business or even at a certain set period. However, one can set a timeline and work towards meeting the set target without having to achieve a specific point, which might turn to be the opposite. To achieve your goals, some points are process-oriented and help in reaching the high note in forex trading and are outlined.

Outline Daily Activities

Day to day activities can only be achieved when put down on paper for a specific task in forex trading. Having in mind the right thing to do on a specific day is good as it helps in avoiding distractions and other things that may come in between a business day. This means that the more you know what you are doing on a busy day, you will not waste time doing other things that do not help achieve your goal and the needs you want to build your forex trading skills.

Analyze the Market

As pointed out earlier, trading with emotions is bad for business as it does not go by the plans and strategy, but with the reaction of business gone wrong or even a big win. Being greedy is so bad in forex trading, and it is advisable to analyze the market first before trying out forex trading and giving a shot on the most promising patterns. When you play by the rules, you train the mind to follow the right procedures and even helps in becoming more discipline in forex trading. Training the mind helps in a vulnerable situation, which will make you hold on when there is a crisis.

2. Be Defensive

This is another important rule to follow in forex trading, for it is the core purpose of joining the business and what will keep you survive storms that will come your way in one way or the other. This simply means that you should not trade everything, including your capital, defend your initial capital, and aim at making profits. When you make a target and do not meet it, then at least you tried, but trading profusely just to meet the target with limited time is not good at all, as it is an offensive approach.

You should always protect your capital as it is the only thing keeping you in the business, and one mistake can send you to factory reset, i.e., going back to the drawing board wondering when the rain started beating you.

3. Have a Trading Plan

Just like any other venture, Forex trading needs a business plan that has been tested to be working and giving impressive results. The plan involves things that you need to do from A-Z. This may include the rules of engagement, trading pattern, market analysis, and other key aspects that make the business run well. After making the trading plan, you can test it virtually to see if it will go well with the market and if it is good, then give it the green light and start the forex trading. But make sure that you outline the plan as it is the backbone of the whole venture.

4. Know That Trading Is a Business

Forex trading is like a business and should be treated as such for one to get the best out of it by giving the attention it deserves. Other researches have talked about not comparing trading with job opportunities or hobby to be done in leisure time. This means that one must not expect a salary and work on getting profits and paying attention and not only focusing on it when you are free. With this, a forex trader will learn to prioritize forex trading just like any other business.

5. Outline Risk

Make sure that you point out the risk you intend to get yourself into and do not give it too much until you are out of business. Do not risk an amount that you cannot afford. Risking is only for the amount you are capable of and not anywhere near initial capital. Remember, as said earlier, if you lose capital, that means that you are out of business, and you will not want that to happen to you. Only risk an amount that you know if they go, then you will not struggle with bringing back the business into living.

6. Use Technology

The modern era of inventions and innovations can be a plus in forex trading as it helps improve the outcome of a venture. Technology has played a big role in forex trading, thanks to innovators who come with new things every day to enhance the world in bringing people closer. With technology, one can trade anywhere in the world monitor charts using a computer or even mobile phones. This means that one can travel all over the world as well as working at the same time. This has been evident for bloggers and travel entrepreneurs who blog for a living and promote products online while they travel. This can be the same for forex traders, and it helps in even having a good time and relaxing the mind while working.

7. Have a Stop-Loss

This is somehow similar to outlining risk but specifies the amount that one should be willing to lose in particular trading. In Forex trading, you should only lose what you afford, and it is very important to outline the amount or percentage that one should only lose in trading. This also acts as a disciplined mode as it helps in controlling the mind and emotions not to surpass the limited amount of possible risk.

8. Focus on the Bigger Picture

What is the purpose of starting forex trading? Can you do the business to be aligned in that direction? Are you getting some profits and losing sometimes? Then you are on the right track heading to greatness in forex trading. Business is not about just making profits but making impacts on a personal level and getting more skills. So what is your bigger picture? To have gained at least 10 percent in the financial year 2019-2020? Having this in mind, then you can be sure of aiming in the right way as compared to only focusing on maximizing profits.

9. Keep Learning Markets

Forex trading is an ongoing process even after mastering markets and getting out of an amateur venture. One does not stop learning at anything, and things keep changing in the forex world. This is important to keep an open mind in everything to do with business. Some of the skilled forex traders can fall prey to crowd psychology, and some markets are unpredictable, making forex trading a learning experience every time one is trading.

10. Be a Progressive Trader

Every forex trader wants to earn profit as it is the main reason for venturing in forex trading in the first point, but are you only profit-oriented the first day in the market, or are you moving forward? Learning also can be huge progress as it helps one avoid making similar mistakes and open ways for more profit in the future. A progressive trade is the one that celebrates every win, either small or big, so long as it is a victory. Just like a child, they learn to sit, then the next thing is they start crawling, and with no time, they start walking with few steps and eventually even running. This is the case to forex trading, you move from one stage to the other, and you cannot jump to only making profits. After making a trading plan and testing it, one can join the trading business and encounter ups and downs as it shapes the ultimate goal of forex trading. With this progress, one can be sure of securing a future in forex trading full of experiences and lots of encounters that can prepare you for any hard hurdles that one might come across at the course of trading.

So, are you setting up your mind on winning and achieving your goals? Then you better follow the procedures outlined above by winning small until you master the art of forex trading and eventually smile to the bank after meeting your ultimate goals. Remember that forex trading is not a walk in the park, so you should make the right choices.

CHAPTER 11:

Common Mistakes and Tips for Beginners in Forex Trading

The forex market, due to its low restriction, makes it one of the most available markets in the world. With an internet connection, phone or computer, and some few dollars, you can begin trading in the market. However, because of its free accessibility does not mean it is easy to make huge returns. When I started trading, I made some of these mistakes, and you have the chance to learn from my mistake. For a fact, I will be saving you thousands of dollars you may have squandered.

Common Forex Mistakes

Mistakes in forex are unavoidable, but there are always remedies to deal with such a situation. Before you consider plunging into trading, it is important to consider the following mistakes and do everything possible to avoid them in the future. Most people are persuaded to venture into forex trading with fantasies of getting rich overnight.

Undeniably, the opportunities in the forex market are innumerable for you to make money and live the lifestyle you want. Notwithstanding, the forex road is not an easy road to travel because it is full of bumps. If there is anything I can assure you as a beginner is that you will struggle for various reasons, including having a poor forex foundation, poor trading structure, and impatience.

These common mistakes cripple the confidence of most beginners. I could boast that you have a solid foundation if you went through the beginning of this book to the end. However, how you apply the principles in this book depends on you only.

These mistakes are the reasons most traders consider the market a scam. I am sure your testimony will be different because you are learning from the best book on forex trading.

Tips for Trading Forex

Just as I promised you at the beginning of this book, to help you avoid the mistake I made as a beginner, I have decided to compile most mistake beginners as you make. I will expound on the top trading tips you should inculcate into your trading and improve your performance.

Learning to trade successfully in the forex market is quite problematic for new traders. Most traders have the mindset of getting rich overnight, which is not something realistic. Forex trading can be prodigious, particularly if you are a beginner and do not know the rules guiding the market. These tips will help you in your trading journey as a beginner. It is always advisable not to forget the basics because, without them, you will struggle in the market.

Pick Your Broker Cleverly

If you can choose the right broker, then you are halfway done in the forex market before choosing any broker. Ensure to seek recommendations from professional traders and do your own research because some traders will recommend a particular broker because of their affiliate programs. Take your time as we have various fake brokers looking for traders like you to ripe off. Do not be moved by mouthwatering deals. Rather look for an authorized broker with years of accomplishment.

Develop Your Strategy

A list of tips on forex trading is not complete without mentioning strategy. As a beginner, you need to create your own trading strategy that works for you. Every trader should know what to expect and get from the market. You should set a definite goal because it will help discipline yourself when trading.

Learn Slowly

Forex is not something you learn and stop over time. Every new skill requires consistent learning to grasp the basics. Additionally, you do not have to rush your learning process. Take your time slowly and begin by investing a little amount of money. Remember that slow and steady will win the race as a beginner.

Control Your Emotions

If you allow your emotions to guide you when trading, you will regret it later. I am not telling you that it is easy, but you can control it. You need to stay rational in order to make wise choices during trading. If you let your emotions rule over you, you are bound to expose yourself to pointless risks. Forex trading is risky, but you can control the level of risk that can happen.

Do Not Trade If You Are Under Stress

Hardly can you see someone who concentrates optimally when under stress. Traders who decide to do that will surely make an irrational decision, which will cost them money. Therefore, before thinking of trading, ensure to identify anything that will cause stress and eliminate them before it eliminates your forex account (do not mind me; I am just joking, but there is a sense to it). If you had a stressful day and still had to trade, consider taking a deep breath while allowing your mind to focus on what you are about to do. You can overcome stress in various ways such as exercising, sleeping, and listening to music, hanging out with friends. Whatever the situation is, find a solution to your stress and manage it effectively.

Never Stop Practicing

Do not neglect this tip because it is crucial to your success or failure as a forex trader. Hardly can you succeed on your first encounter in the forex market. Therefore, when you make your first mistake, do not relent because, with consistent practicing, you will be among the top traders. However, you have the adventure of using a demo account to perfect your skill.

Risk Is Part of the Game

If you are not ready to risk, you are not ready for the forex market. Most brokers will advise you that trading is risky, and you should accept that fact. If you think that in forex you are going to have a sweet ride, then you need a reality check. Additionally, I have seen mouthwatering advertisements promising you the "unpromising." Well, you should be realistic about your goals and strategies.

Patience Is Priceless

Do you remember the old adage? “True success is never instantaneous.” That holds true in the forex market. It is the product of consistent planning and work, which many beginners tend to overlook. There is no easy path to making a profit in the market. Let patience have her way in you.

Upgrade Your Knowledge Continuously

The more you trade, the newer things you learn. Improve your knowledge by looking at trends, analyzing news, and financial processes. Furthermore, do not neglect the fundamental basis you have learned. Significantly, you should study, practice, and continue this routine. A knife gets dull when it is left idle. Sharpen your trading skill with continuous learning and practicing.

Take Breaks

All work and no play makes Jack a dull student. You can take routine breaks, especially when you are under stress. For those glued to multiple computer winds to analyze data from various sources, it is important to take a break as you may feel pressured.

Trends Are Essential

Trends are important for any trader, and you should not neglect them. The capability to identify these trends makes it a valuable investment for you. I understand there are various trends; it is important to ignore those that will lead to disaster. Trends give you a picture of what may come in the future. With this, you can prepare for the future.

Planning Is a Necessary Ingredient

Forex trading is not sports betting where you gamble the team to win or score. Forex trading is a strategic game that requires painstaking planning and attention to evaluate your next move before taking action. Before starting any trade, formulate a plan that includes challenging questions like:

- What is my primary plan?
- What is plan B?
- What strategy should I employ?
- What are my loss and profit margins?

Understand the Charts

You will trade in various markets, and these require different information to analyze each trade. We have numerous tools you can use to make your trading easier. However, charts are time efficient and serve as the best option for beginners. You should not know them only. You should learn how to read and use them to your advantage.

Incorporate Stop-Losses in Your Trades

Setting stop-loss for trade is an efficient strategy to use when trading. With stop-loss, you minimize your risk and escape any trade that goes haywire. Additionally, avoid greediness by setting the maximum profit and loss range. Once you hit your target, you should avoid the trap of placing another trade.

CHAPTER 12:

Options Trading Terminology

- **Ask price:** This is the lowest price that is being advertised in the options trading that anyone is willing to accept when selling a particular option at a particular period.

- **At the money:** This term is used to describe the nearest price to the equity price during a particular trading moment.

- **Bearish:** This term, on the other hand, describes a trader who believes that the market prices will do lower or the market will experience a downfall at particular trading activity in a specific period.

- **Bid spread:** This is the actual difference between the asking price and the bid price for a given option during a particular options trading period.

- **Big chicken trade:** This is a term used to describe a series of bull call calendars, and the bear put calendars.

- **Break-even point:** This is the specific price that an underlying asset must reach to avoid the option buyer from acquiring losses if at all, they decided to exercise the option.

- **Bullish:** This term is particularly referring to an investor who believes that a specific stock price will go higher or simply the market will rise higher.

- **Call option:** This is an equity agreement that awards a buyer the chance to purchase 100 particular shares at a particular strike price within a specified time. A seller is also needed to sell off the stock at a particular price if the option gets exercised.

- **Credit:** It is any value amount received in a particular trading account from the financial benefits experienced in various options trading activities. The profits and multiple benefits feed the trading accounts.

- **Change:** The percentage term price of the last hour's sale in the options market.

- **Commission:** This is the fee charged in an options trading market after option orders have been executed on a securities exchange.

- **Contract:** This is an agreement set between a buyer trader and a seller trader during a particular options trading activity.

- **Credit:** It is any value amount received in a particular trading account from the financial benefits experienced in various options trading activities. The profits and multiple benefits feed the trading accounts.

- **Debit:** This is any amount of cash paid out to purchase an option during a particular trading period.

- **Dip in the money:** This is a term used to refer to multiple in-the-money occurrences that have been experienced in a particular trading period in the options market.

- **Downside risk:** This is the estimation of a particular downfall market price that is likely to be experienced by the market during the end of a particular trading period.

- **Equity option:** It is a kind of option that gives the owner, who happens to be the buyer, the chance to purchase and sell any available stock in the trading market at a specific share during a particular period before the expiration date is reached.

- **Ex-dividend:** This is the actual date in which the stock enters the options trading market with the absence of dividends.

- **Expiry date:** This is the actual date–day, month, or year–to which a particular option trading contract becomes invalid and null.

- **Front-month:** When the expiration of two months is involved in options trading, the month nearer in time is normally considered.

- **Historical volatility:** This is analyzing the actual volatility of the past market occurrences and making the necessary helpful strategies and learning in your trading plan.

- **Holder:** The specific owner of the contract is referred to as the holder in options trading.

- **Horizontal:** This is a term describing the options of the same strike price experienced in different months.

- **Implied volatility:** This is an estimation of the future likelihood market volatility by analyzing the market status through the current activities occurring at the options trading market. Some traders get to use this as one of their strategies the options trading market to acquire large chunks of profits.

- **Index option:** This is an option contract where the index is the underlying stock and not shares of any specific stock.
- **In the money:** All the strike prices possess some intrinsic value where for a call, all strike prices are below the equity price, whereas, for a put, all prices are the ones above the price of the equity.
- **Last sale:** It is the latest price that a certain option trader has traded within options trading.
- **Long Option:** This simply implies having purchased an option at online transactions and therefore own it.
- **Margin:** This is a particular amount of loan offered by a particular broker of a specific trader during a particular trading period.
- **Mean:** This is a mathematical operation where the total sum of observations in the market is divided by the particular number of observations

in the market. The mean is used to provide data on various market values and the market standard deviation.

- **Open interest:** This is the number of the option that has been sold and also the ones that have not been brought back or, in any case, exercise.

- **Option:** It is a contract that allows an investor to purchase and sell a specific trading stock at a particular price within a particular period.

- **Option spread:** It is established by buying and selling equal amounts of options of a similar class with the same underlying security. However, the strike prices and expiration dates of the options are different.

- **Premium:** This is the amount of income received by an option trader as he or she writes a contract off to another party.

- **Put option:** The kind of option where a buyer is given the privilege to sell 100 shares at a constant price before the expiration date. On the other hand, the seller of a put option is required to purchase stock at a particular price if the trading option gets exercised at all.

- **Resistance:** This is a particular level where the equity price cannot beyond any way higher, meaning that that particular price is the actual price limit.

- **Selling to open:** This ideally describes the selling of a particular option to open a position.

- **Selling to close:** Selling a close means selling a specific option with the desire to close a particular position during options trading.

- **Short Option:** This means to have sold the option in an opening transaction.

- **Stock:** It is described as a portion of a particular company belonging or ownership.

- **Spread:** This is an option position established when a purchase of one option is established and a sale of an option too using the same underlying asset available in the trading market.

- **Strike price**: This is the actual amount of price in which you choose to sell or buy options when you decide to exercise an option in the market.

- **Time decay:** This is the erosion period when the value of time of a specific option diminishes as the expiration date reaches.

- **Time value:** It describes the value to which time is attributable in options before a particular expiration date is reached.

- **Trading platform:** This is a general trading site that traders interact with while making trading moves, buying, selling, and any other trading activities. Trading platforms consist of various kinds according to different variety of interests, and a trader gets to pick on a site in which he or she is most comfortable with.

- **Underlying asset:** This is the 100 shares of stock that are involved in a particular agreement during a specified time.

- **Vertical:** It is a term describing the options of different strike prices experienced in a particular month.

- **Volatility:** This is the actual fluctuation of prices of stocks in options trading where the stock prices keep rising and falling within time hence making it hard for traders to predict likely future activities.

- **Volume:** This is the number of contracts that have been traded during a particular options trading period.

- **Writing an option:** This is to sell a call or put option contract that has been not possessed by any other trader in the market.

Conclusion

IIf you are reading this, congratulations on going through the book. At the end of this book, you have been able to get in-depth knowledge of the craft of day trading. You no longer have to question what day trading is and how to go about it.

If you are a newbie day trader, the book has given you numerous tips and guidelines to become a successful trader. Probably at the start, you did not know what instrument to trade-in. However, now you know about day trading in stocks, forex, or cryptocurrencies. The details in this book should be able to help you improve as a newbie trader or give you the motivation and information to start day trading.

Maybe you have always wondered if you can do a profitable business out of day trading. If this has been your dilemma, it doesn't need to be anymore. You now know it is possible to do business in day trading and earn your daily living.

Having all the equipment you need to trade is important. The book emphasized these things, and now you know where to begin. You don't have to procrastinate anymore but take a chance now and begin your day trading career.

Have your personal goals and strategies that you tie together with your day trading strategies and take the risk. Just like any other venture in life, day trading takes a risk, and, in most cases, it pays off handsomely.

Forex trading is not for everyone. You should never trade what you cannot afford to lose. Besides, you should be committed to keeping your emotions out of your trading decisions while making smart decisions based on facts.

If Forex trading is for you, then it is important to set realistic expectations. Even the very best traders like Warren Buffet only increased their portfolio by 20 percent a year, while most hedge fund managers are thrilled to grow their portfolios by 10 percent a year.

There are many approaches to Forex trading. Your personality, your available time, and your ability to read market indicators all play important factors in determining the best approach for you. Regardless of your approach, however, it is important to think before you trade as statistics show that the best way to lose money in Forex trading is to trade too often.

If you wanted to learn how you could make money efficiently and make huge profits by investing only small amounts of money, we have shown you that you should choose to invest in the stock market. There are only some people who know how to invest in the stock market because they have learned how to do so. If you follow the information in this book, you can learn how to do this too. You will gather plenty of information about stocks and the different types of stocks you can invest in. This book also sheds some light on the different techniques you can use to invest in stocks.

As a beginner, you may make mistakes when you start investing in stocks. This is absolutely fine because you will start off with a small amount of money. But you cannot do this in the future because you will tend to invest larger amounts of money. It is important that you always learn from the mistakes that you make. Remember, every experienced trader also made mistakes at the start, but they always learned from their mistakes. It is this experience that will help you do well in the market.

All the best!

CPSIA information can be obtained
at www.ICGtesting.com
Printed in the USA
LVHW050937280621
691317LV00013BA/518